Leading Bharat

Dev Raval

KORYFI GROUP
of Media & Publications

Leading Bharat

Author: Dev Raval

ISBN: 978-81-988214-5-4

Price: Rs. 120/-

First Published in October, 2025

Publisher & Printer:

Koryfi Group of Media and Publications
Address: B-515, 5th Floor, Shalin Square, Nr. Lalgebi Circle,
S. P. Ring Road, Hathijan, Ahmedabad, Gujarat, India - 382445
Phone: +91-635 635 60 70 | **Email:** editor@koryfigroup.org
Website: book.koryfigroup.org

Leading Bharat Preface

This book is all about my vision and views on our Bharat which is society by than and now.as its title says "**leading Bharat**", is in my life not just a book but a vision with a mission to see Bharat as a leading country in every aspect on global platforms. I as a youth of the country at the age of fifteen have tried to pen down every angle be it past, present and the future for our leading Bharat. Also, every chapter is worth reading as it is my depthful study and research work which am sure every reader would admire as well as acknowledge too. Also have shared my suggestive views towards how the youth of Bharat views a "**leading Bharat**".

Table of Content

Ch. 1: The History of India and How it was Designed to work **01**

Section-1: How India Was Made to Work 01

Section-2: History of Uprising of India 01

Section-3: The Ideal Government Structure According To Our Pre-Independence Leaders 02

Ch. 2: A Foreign Ideal Policy for India **04**

Section-1: India's Foreign Policy Before Freedom 04

Section-2: India's Foreign Policy Under Inc-Upa Government 05

Section-3: India's Foreign Policy Under Bjp-Nda Government 06

Section-4: an Ideal Foreign Policy for India 07

Ch. 3: Ideal defence policy for India **09**

Section-1: The Past Leadership for Defence in India 09

Section-2: The Present Leadership for Defence in India 10

Section-3: The Ideal Leadership for Defence India 11

Ch. 4: Ideal Financial System for India **12**

Section-1: The Past Financial Policy Under Inc and Upa Government 12

Section-2: The Present Financial Policy by Bjp-Nda Government 12

Section-3: The Ideal Financial Policy For India 12

Ch. 5: Ideal Judicial System for India **15**

Section-1: The Past and The Present Court Trials in India 15

Section-2: The Solution and Ideal System for Judiciary and its Trials in India 15

Ch. 6: Ideal Education System for India **17**

Section-1: Educational System Under British Rule 17

Section-2: Education System Under the Real Indian Culture 17

Section-3: Ideal Education System for India 18

Ch. 7: Is Holding of Elections Proper in India **20**

Section-1: Correct Way for Holding Elections in India 20

Section-2: Malpractices Taking Place Elections in India 21

Ch. 8: An Advisory for Citizens to Choose a Perfect Leader **23**

Ch. 9: All The Strengths and Weaknesses of our Country and How to Work on Them **24**

Section-1: The Strengths of India 24

Section-2: Weaknesses of India 25

Section-3: How to Overpower our Weaknesses 26

Ch. 10: An Ideal Way of Leading Bharat **27**

Refrences of Leading Bharat 28

Ch. 1
The History of India and The Ideal Way How it Was Designed to Work

This chapter will give a short recap on the history of India and the ideal structure designed by the leaders of India for its working process.

Section 1: How India Was Made to Work

the beginning of Indian revolution started far earlier than our independence unlike the other revolutions, India got its freedom a bit late. From the starting of the revolution or the revolt of 1857,the key features of this were fighting against the provocation of Indian people and also on fighting against the censorship law ,which was brought by the east India company.aguriculturists of India also fought for their equal wages ,which were not fulfilled by the British rule, the east India company massacred a number of Indian people who fought against them, and the freedom fighters of India also maintained a peaceful protest against the government ,but many radicals also fought a separate war with weapons, all together got us the freedom and our birthright of living in our own sovereign, secular, socialist democratic country.

Section 2: History of Uprising of India

in the section one of the chapter, we came to know how India fought the freedom struggle but this part also gave us a key prospect that how India was to work after getting freedom. Now, let's rewind ourselves to the revolt of 1857 the key reason for that revolt was that both the Hindu and the Muslim refused to use the new cartridges of the British rule. But the key thing which we missed was that instead of fighting separately both Hindu and Muslim fought together against the rule so, the pre-independent India (except the later Muslim league of Jinnah) was a willing a government which would be totally on oppose of the relational politics, which unfortunately we can see after the freedom. Now let's go to the second key prospect of the pre-independent India, the British government brought vernacular press act of 1878 which was made to stop newspapers, articles from publishing against the British government and directly after this law passed in parliament and protest started. Newspaper channels instead of stopping to publish started largely to publish more-and-more articles and pages against the British government. There were also many Indians who did not support the freedom struggle, but were on a good post in the British government, but the newspaper channels also did not hesitate to publish against those fellow Indians. this point is not directly linked with what I'm about to tell, but does connect with it. now in the government of today there is freedom for press but, there are some channels and newspaper channels which do glorify either indirectly or in a sort of direct manner to the government or the opposition, if we go by evidence the India before independence had a press which worked to give the correct information to the people and not for glorifying any leader who was involved in the freedom struggle. The press in the late and last years of British rule also encouraged many good deeds done viceroy lord Mountbatten because he was working to give correct information not one-sided information and not for glorification of leaders, the true press should work for giving the promise for providing right information to the citizens so that they can choose an ideal leader instead or misleading them.

Section 3: The Ideal Government Structure According to Our Pre-Independence Leaders

now, as we have saw in this book previous sections that how we in our pre-freedom stage wanted our country to be ruled now let's see a perfect structuring of the Indian government (by our thinking for an ideal country before our freedom.

press

should be free and should work without any pressure a leader or any party and should work for providing right information

socialism, secularism

there should be no sort of religional politics and discrimination in people. All citizens should strife equal rights on their merit

India shall be peaceful but India will also use weapons if it's on our countries pride and self-respect

Ch. 2
A Foreign Ideal Policy for India

The first two sections of this chapter will provide the information about the foreign policies of the past and present governments of India. and the last section and the most intresting one will provide information on what be a ideal foreign policy.

Section 1: India's Foreign Policy Before Freedom
in our early stage after independence India and its leaders had a definite and decided foreign policy leaders, such as Nehru and Gandhi had a stand on being independent and also preferred a great stance in the trading and selling of 'swadeshi' or India's own produced cloth 'khadi' and many other things which included spices etcetera however had a stand of government where he opposed imperialism and proposed a close alignment with soviet union and appreciating its geopolitical moves , but he also maintained peaceful stand for world and promised to ensure world peace. India maintained a close tie-up with soviets as they helped India in various prospects, however they eventually saw their own profits too, but maintaining close relations with soviet union was done because of USA's direct increasing interests in Pakistan, India also had started an initiative of trading with south Asian states like African countries in-order to boost Indian economy relations with China were stable before the Nehru's visit to China as China was directly interested in the north western territories of India and wished to invade them, which leaded to the Indochinese war of 1962,which had a direct effect on India's foreign policy whose effects can be still be seen in India's relations with China.

at first India had a strict stand of not supporting any superpower and supported decolonization of states all over the world.

Section 2: India's Foreign Policy Under Inc-Upa Government

A. ERA FROM 1947-1964

if we start from the first feature of inc government (1947-1964) firstly as we discussed India maintained (Nam) or non-alignment movement also, India Toke a strong stand in abolishment of colonies majorly in the south-Asian parts of the world which also included south Africa in 1961. India in its post-independent period maintained a non-support agreement with blocs of superpower countries, India also signed 'panchsheel' agreement with China which included non-aggression from both sides. however, this agreement was later been broken by China. The war of 1962 led India then for making close relations with superpowers like Ussr, where us posed a mixed state and leaned more towards Pakistan as an ally. Meanwhile in the 1950s India also intervened in the case of Korea promoting un's peace making trials.

B. ERA FROM 1966-1977

under the rule of Indira Gandhi, the biggest move for the foreign policy in which India signed the agreement indo-soviet agreement of peace of friendship and co-operation where Ussr aided India with military support during the indo-pak war of 1971, Indira Gandhi government also was a pro-nuclear armament government which conducted the pokhran-1 test.

C. ERA 1984-1989

under prime minister Rajiv Gandhi Indian forces were sent to Sri Lanka. this force was known as (ipkf) or the Indian peace keeping force in (1987-1990) under indo-sri Lankan accord. also, India intervened in the military coup of Maldives taking place in 1988, while also liberalized economy in order to attract foreign investment, while this government also maintained close relations with Soviet Union.

D. ERA FROM 1991-1996

in the era of pv. Narsimha Rao, as of the collapse of Soviet Union India faced many economic losses in which India also attained close relations with Israel and, also tried to improve relations with united states of America, while tensions with Pakistan still stayed a great issue to deal with

E. ERA FROM 2004-2014

under the upa government led by Manmohan Singh India signed indo-us nuclear treaty which unbaled for getting civil nuclear fuel and technology from us while, also maintaining strong ties with the Russian federation in defence industry. India also joined brics in 2009 which made a great economic boostage.

Section 3: India's Foreign Policy Under Bjp-Nda Government

A. ERA FROM 1998-2004

under the Atal Bihari Vajpayee, India conducted pokhran-2 nuclear test which made India a nuclear state, but this move invited many sanctions by the west.in this era India also maintained strong ties with Russia and also condemned 9/11 terror attacks on us, which led to a boost in strength of India with USA, while also solving the indo-Chinese border issue partially after the Kargil war of 1999

B. ERA FROM 2014-AT PRESENT (AS OF 2025)

the Modi government tried to ensure both maintaining relations with us and Russia while also dealing with Japan. but the tariff issue of 2025 and Chinese border issue also remained enact where us 'penelted' India for buying crude oil from Russia.

Section 4: An Ideal Foreign Policy for India

for ideal foreign policy for India, we should remember all the way back from our freedom till at present. India is a agriculturist country and we are totally dependent on it the increasing tariffs by USA could directly affect the farmers of our country but India should also keep in mind that we also enforce a very hefty amount of tax on other nations which of almost (varying from 15% to 300%) India charges 50% tax on automobiles which also results in our loss and their loss who exports, as we have to buy goods at a very high rate. "If we want to have good than we have to give good" India should reduce this much hefty amount of tax so, that manufacturers and Indian manufacturers get imported raw materials on a decent rate, and also can export them on a decent rate without any foreign taxes. if we lower the tax than we will have a point to defend ourselves that India does not charge high amount of import duties as the xyz country does. also, we should understand one thing that India has got a very long-term relation with Russia and previously the Soviet Union in all terms from defence till trade. "we cannot have the taste of both the cake and laddu at same time" same as that I am not telling to disrupt the relations with the west, but we should understand that we cannot afford Russia to go against us and I remember the quote of out external affairs minister Mr Jaishankar that " Europe's problems are world's problems but world's problems are not Europe's problems" us always has been taking profitable stance for their own benefit and has not should interest in maintaining relations with any country example Pakistan after the withdrawal of us forces in Afghanistan it does not help or aid Pakistan anymore but they do maintain their long term friendship with Israel samely we have our long term ally Russia. almost 90% defence equipment of India is imported from Russia. that's why India should not de-satisfy Russia for any other country's relations also remember that when f1 came to India Uttar Pradesh government made a 1500 crore rupee budh circuit in Uttar Pradesh, but then because of corruption up government told f1 as an entertainment and not as a sport while whole world considers formula one races as a sport. after that they enforce a high amount of taxes on f1 because of this their equipment had to be stuck in customs till many weeks. then f1 Toke India out from there race schedule. if f1 would still be there now it, might have created a great amount of economic benefit to India in various prospects. also, if we now show a light on indo-Chinese conflict India should be strong and declare a definite line of control (loc) with China. we can stop their imports to India for 6 months; indeed, this would affect India but we are also among the biggest markets of Chinese goods which would affect China more than usa and meanwhile we would also start filling the gap of Chinese goods by our own. China can't afford a war with India. by this India can pressure China to stop proclaiming and illegally invading territories of India. this method will resolve the indo-China border issue permanently but India will need a strong leadership to do so. these were the points which I think will lead to ideal foreign policy for present and future of India.

Ch. 3
Ideal Defence and Military Leadership for India

Section 1: The Past Leadership For Defence In India

India from its pre-independence period has been on one stand that India is a peace-loving nation but if someone tries to break its harmony of peace India also knows to use weapons. from the revolt of 1857 till the making of 'Azad hind fauj' or the Indian national army (Ina) by Subhash Chandra Bose we always have proven ourselves on battlefield for the safety of peace. at the time on Ina they had their leader Subhash Chandra Bose, Marathas had their leader Chhatrapati Shivaji Maharaj. by this we conclude that leadership also plays a vital and crucial role in defence. now if we rewind back to 1971 Indira Gandhi as a pm was a strong leader too, I am not telling this on any party's support but at that time, India was not that strong as it is now and we had geopolitical pressure from many superpowers. The west totally should their alignment with Pakistan. Pakistan was gifted by USA with f-104 starfighter jets one of best and fastest at that time, while India didn't have that much defence equipment for direct compaction. the only power which India had was that our leadership was strong, yes Ussr with India after the indo-soviet treaty of peace. But the most of battle was to fought by India, Soviet Union only handled the external military pressures, but the internal between India and Pakistan had to fought by India, because of strong leadership our army handled more than 90,000 troops on the eastern front made them to surrender with the biggest amount of army surrender ever taking place in world only and only because of strong leadership. If at that time our leadership had stayed enact and do nothing, Pakistan might have massacred many people and also, we would always had had to fight Pakistan from two fronts. pressures on every developing country by the superpowers but it's how it's the leaderships response how to handle it on their way. yes, I am indeed not a supporter of war but peace also comes at a cost which we have to pay for the safety of our country after the war sanctions on India stayed but got resolved after time healed itself but if we hadn't taken that move India might would be facing its costs till now. the r&aw or the research and analysis wing of India has given many warnings before many major attacks on India but all most all the government has not taken them seriously and we have paid the cost of many deaths of our citizens. like the 26/11 Mumbai attacks and ic 814 plane hijacking.

Section 2: The Present Leadership for Defence in India

the present leadership was considered a powerful leadership, of its response in Uri and Pulwama attacks. but if we rewind back to five days before the Pahal gam attacks r&aw gave a warning to the central government that a major attack can take place in the region of Kashmir, but the central leadership Toke it as a normal whistle blower or a rumour rather than considering it as a legitimate warning. and then we again saw the results. After that whole country wished war on Pakistan but india just did an operation in which we only destroyed some terrorist camps of lashkar. now let's keep people's emotions on side and go practically and statistically, Pakistan and its terrorist friends have been attacking India's civilians and military personnel from many years and sheltering terrorist camps. if Pakistan feared our operations, they would not dare to attack india. but Pakistan does not fear now if india doesn't take a severe action this will become a never-ending process and also attract many tensions. Most severe among them stays Kashmir which will lose many economic benefits because of lower tourism. Common public of Kashmir would get in economic crisis and would face routine cross-border firings of artillery guns, which also destroy many infrastructures of india in Kashmir. so, the leadership should take a big and long-lasting move rather than just affecting temporary losses to our enemy.

Section 3: The Ideal Leadership for Defence India

the ideal leadership for defence in india should firstly stop fearing of geopolitical pressures, india is a powerful country that we do not need any kind of interference in our matters by the west. firstly, they cannot declare any major decision of defence ministry of india or neither they should be allowed to interfere in our national conflict. Secondly as I mentioned before we can see many problems caused by Pakistan's actions to india. we also have to face many civilian and infrastructural losses because of their actions. so, the first thing india should completely resolve the issue of Pakistan by completely taking over Pakistan. I am not emotionally speaking but after the WW2 USA and its allies and Ussr completely Toke control of German territory and kept it under them till many years after the disintegration of Ussr USA and its allies declared Germany as a separate country, but they also did establish a situation that Germany could never try to create a mess for them again. we can take over Pakistan and amend our constitution in a way that Pakistan only should be directly under presidential control and no common citizen from india and the same for their citizens shall visit there without prior permission. we can also free up the Baloch movement by giving them their territory and after curtain years if needed than we can declare Pakistan independent again by establishing a puppet government there which would allow no sort of terrorist camps to build there. This will completely solve many problems for india like interference of our other enemies there will be stopped Kashmir will reunite, and the threat of terrorist attacks from there will be stopped permanently. yes, our army navy and air force are that capable to do such operation but yes for that india needs a strong leadership to do so as we can destroy terrorist camps but not terrorism.

Ch. 4
Ideal Financial System for India

Section 1: The Past Financial Policy Under Inc and Upa Government

the inc-upa government majorly focused on scheme such as mgnrega (2005) which guaranteed lifting over two million people out of poverty with a fiscal deficit hit of 6% in 2009-2010.inc- upa government also focussed on food security and subsidised food for below poverty population, also liberalization for (fdi) or foreign direct investment in retail and insurance boosting. the inc-upa government also introduce Aadhaar card system, but later faced many challenges of funds and corruption.

Section 2: The Present Financial Policy by Bjp-Nda Government

the bjp and bjp-nda government has been majorly focussing on prospects such as digitalisation such as the upi model (which handles global transactions of more than 50%) and also launched (dbt) or direct benefit transfers (three lakh crores annually). this government also launched social welfare schemes as pm kisan yojana. also launched Ayushman Bharat, they also carried on the idea of Aadhaar card by the inc-upa government. the consolidated fiscal deficits of the government were about 3.5% of the GDP in financial years 2023-2024 and also did demonetisation of bank notes, however this also phased criticism on economic disruptions by de-monetisation and coverage issues in Ayushman scheme.

Section 3: The Ideal Financial Policy for India

india is a vast country with a very huge amount of population; we have to handle both global and national sectors. india has a total budget of 50.65 lakh crores (approx. every year) and for example let's see a pie-chart on financial budget of 2025-26 of our earning from direct sectors

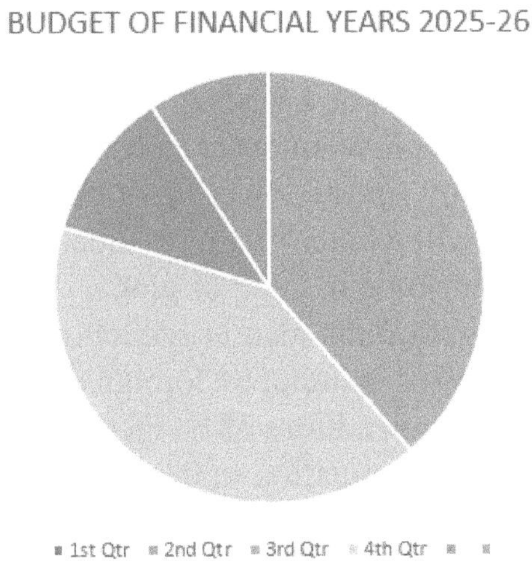

A. income tax-22%
B. 24% borrowing and other liabilities
C. 1% non-debt capital receipts
D. 4% non-tax receipts
E. 17% co-operation tax
F. 5% union excise duties
G. 18% gst and other taxes

now, let's firstly focus on earnings, then we can see that union excise duties contributes 5% union excise duties which is about 2,53,250 crores of rupees, but we also now are facing the tariffs from USA which are increasing (10% rough estimate of fiscal deficit) now, if we do take the 5% of union excise duties to 1.5 or 2% then this tax reduction will directly increase the earning from liabilities such as exporting. because if we reduce the duties then the importing companies will have decent profits because of this that country from which the things are imported such as tesla for ex will setup more and more plants in india and then for ex if tesla model x costs of 65 lakhs after duties it will directly reduce to 35 lakhs actual cost.so, the demand for cars, bikes and other imported material will increase rapidly. After this the government can charge 2.79% tax as automobile tax this tax will be charged on citizens of their total investment in cars for ex if one person has two cars, and on both he has spent 20 lakhs so the tax costed will 2.79% of the total investment which will 2.79% of 20 lakhs which is about 55,800 riposte lowering of duties and availability of raw materials will result in more independent production which will also contribute in GDP or global domestic product of India. This will benefit india also in reduction of tariffs or taxes charged on our exported material by foreign countries. Now, if we observe the internal expenditure of budget on schemes etc. india has a great amount of population to deal with and as the number of populations increases their problems and needs also increase. Almost 11.28% of the total population of india (approx.) stays below poverty line, if the problem of below poverty population has to be solved, we will need a survey of exact margins that how many people stay like this. then we can sectorise their problems and needs in different categories and the focus of government should be on providing employment because employment can solve almost all issues of a person. now how to do that right, most of employment providing schemes are handled by government till now. if we separately make an employment commission like other commissions and assign it a separate budget and workforce this will enhance the chances of more employment as, if worked is done in a categorised manner it will enhance the efficiency of work, the government should assign an initial budget of 36% to the employment of the total budget then only this issue will be solved for lifetime. But for applying this method india will need a non-corrupt government which shall work for public need and not for their own political desires.

Ch. 5
Ideal Judicial System for India

Section 1: The Past and The Present Court Trials in India
the Indian judicial system is a very strong form of judicial system amongst the world; Indian judicial system stays as an independent branch of the government and is empowered to guide or warn the government if needed without any external interference. the court trials are conducted in india from our pre-independent period and are made in a structure which prevents any of the violation of rules given by our constitution.

Section 2: The Solution and Ideal System for Judiciary and its Trials in India
'Justice delayed is justice denied' a very powerful quote which says if justice is delayed then justice is denied or not served india has a population of 140.09 crores, where every day approx. 5385 criminal cases are filed in courts, only criminal cases and pending cases include more than 45.23 million cases. While there are only 15 judges per million population, also rape cases are filed in india every day the most horrible among them rape case of Delhi the Nirbhaya case was been disposed and complete at time period of 10 years. This kind of a system neither gives justice nor promises to do so as every day crime rate increases and each case has an average disposal period of 5 years and not less than that the correct method to improve this system is to survey the exact number of judges per million people and cases filed per million people. Then we should minimise and set an amount of 100 judges recruited per million people and maximum amount of court trials should be set so that judiciary can promise justice in time to the people

of our country. there should be a separate committee of disposal of cases on time, so that all cases be supervised and cases shall be disposed in a time period of 6 months, yes, I know our population is far greater to deal with but we need a judiciary that should give a security to complete cases in time by using these two methods. Yes, Indian judiciary has opened courts at night to deal with extreme cases but rest of the system stays slow under regional levels and if Indian judiciary cannot fulfil the promise of justice will not be delayed than I am afraid but Indian people will lose the hope of justice by the courts.

Ch. 6
Ideal Education System for India

Section 1: Educational System Under British Rule
so, from our pre-independence era if we rewind back to British rule, the British government ran a system in which regional and cultural educational systems were been abolished which was common in most of their colonies. Till 1947 British built many schools, colleges, universities etc, and also ran projects for educating girls, but the main curriculum of the British government was that compulsory English should be considered as the primary language they also taught Indian children on their perspectives where they were taught of British crown and governance also British curriculum was a propaganda to prioritize English, sciences, literature etc over India's cultural language Sanskrit and Hindi. Because of continuous expansion of British education system in india the vernacular languages of different regions started to neglect as of their propaganda.

Section 2: Education System Under the Real Indian Culture
the real education system comprised of regional based education on various subjects and cultural sciences as mathematics (ganit or Vedic mathematics) sciences like (bhugolvidhya or geography) and history generally from Rigveda and other vedas.it also taught children on chakras or medicine according to Hindu religion, and taught ayurvedic ways of healing and study of bodyparts.in this system students had stay with their gurus in a gurukul to study and examination system was also designed according to guru which varied from student-to-student, this education system was majorly been encouraged by scholars such as swami Vivekanand and

Gandhiji. And this system also made many great mathematicians like Aryabhata the inventor of zero in mathematics.

Section 3: Ideal Education System for India

the most recent education system is mostly similar to the British education system which included studying in school building. There are only some minor changes like edition of vernacular languages but they are also considered as secondary in most of the schools. Government schools also follow the same system the only change is that unlike private schools' government schools consider regional languages as primary. The biggest heritage of india was its education, India in its history has built tremendous universities like the Nalanda university which had over nine million books on various subjects. The biggest propaganda of britishers in their every colony was to brig it away from its culture which I think so, that in india they succeeded to do it.if I take an example of China and Japan they still teach their children according to their respective cultures and they are far more developed than rest of the world so, development does not mean studying in high schools in English language, development can be brought to india if we again start our cultural gurukuls instead of this British system, I think that Indian education should be perceived in our vernacular language and according to our culture. India has far more advanced skills than britishers that was the reason why they weakened our strongest strength out culture. If india starts again the gurukul system with some changes like women should be allowed to perceive education. And remove all examinations like the boards, instead add skill ability and advancement courses also advised by sir Apj Abdul kalam. The redesigning of the whole education system should take place, which should be according to our golden heritage then we shall see the real development in our country.

System for nursery, pri-primary and secondary *education according to our culture*

1. till three years in gurukul curriculum should include Panchatantra stories education
2. primary education in gurukul
3. after each child's performance skill training and explanations according to their opted skills

subjects

1. Sanskrit
2. Hindi
3. Vedic mathematics
4. bhugol geography according to Hindu culture
5. history and heritage
6. ayurvedic methods of healing and study of body parts
7. jyotisa or astronomy i.e. study of universe

Ch. 7
Is Holding of Elections Proper in India

Section 1: Correct Way for Holding Elections in India

India's election system is among the most complex and democratic forms of election processes in the world. The holding of elections in india is controlled by election commission of india or eci which was established in 1950 the election commission of india is considered as most powerful election commissions among the world, which is and independent body of government. Elections in india are hosted on regular time period of 5 years, Lok Sabha and legislative assemblies unless the government dissolves earlier. The election process starts from de-limitation of constituencies where boundaries of electoral constituencies are re-drawn periodically under article 82 of Indian constitution based on census to ensure equal representation. The second step is preparation of electoral rolls (voter registration) in which all the citizens above the age of 18 can register for voting in elections via e-portals and form-6 which can be done offline, then these rolls are designed again under special summery revision or (sir),then the rolls and details of each voter are given to blos or booth level officers, then they do a final revision by going door-to-door to each sector for voter id or (epic) or electors' photo identity card and is been issued and then a voter id card is issued to the voter by using other identification documents such as Aadhaar card etc. The third step includes filing of nominations of the candidates' contesting elections. Their details are stored in forms 2a and 2b with affidavits disclosing assets, criminal records and educational qualifications which has been made mandatory according to 2002 supreme court guidelines. Then nominations are examined for validity. The third step includes campaigning which begins after nominations and stops before 48 hours of poling, according to mic or model for code of conduct this prohibits hate speech, vote buying, and misuse of government resources, an amount is fixed which shall be followed for expenditure in elections in which for Lok Sabha 95 lakhs respectively. The fourth step includes poling held at more than 1 million booths across the country, through evm's or electoral voting machines which are not connected with any sort of internet to prevent hacking. After that the fifth step includes counting of votes, where the evm's are released and transported to secured locations for counting which happens under surveillance under cctv cameras' last step is declaration of results whoever scores highest votes, wins the elections.

Section 2: Malpractices Taking Place Elections in India

if start by steps then there are many electoral malpractices by 2024-25 as questioned by opposition leader Rahul Gandhi that more than 85 thousand duplicate voting in panvel, Mumbai Toke place. The other example is vote buying, according to record of 2024 more than 14,650 crore rupees were been found in Maharashtra which were illegally used in elections. The malpractice stays that most of major news channels are been bribed by big political parties who always show information in there bribing parties favour.an MP of Mumbai Ravindra waiker was accused for using mobile phones in polling booth which is illegal. The most recent example stays that in Gujarat more than 1000 parties approx. were found as ghostly parties because, the parties in this list have never taken part in any form of election yet, these parties receive an average donation of more than 1000 crore rupees which stays more than many central parties, the probability stays that these parties might be working as shell parties for other major parties.yes,india has the most free and fair form of election process.but,are the rules of this system being followed?.is election commission of india responsibly working to safeguard this system and its laws. if so, then why we can see these much amount of electoral scandels. by my thinking a separate organisation shall be formed for supervising the working of ec.and a separate task force should be formed which shall be named security force for polling booths be formed in-order to prevent misuse or violation of rules in polling booths. If our country has to form a separate commission to literally supervise election commission then, we conclude the amount of leisure Ness should by ec in electoral processes.

Ch. 8
An Advisory for Citizens to Choose a Perfect Leader

this, chapter is most important chapter as no one has ever talked of this point in our history in India. From 27 years (approx.) we are witnessing bjp government and before that inc government. Yes, indeed prime minister Narendra Modi is a good leader and Manmohan Singh also was a good leader. But if I take an example of bjp they follow Modi propaganda in which, they tell citizens from legislative to rural elections to vote for Modi, but the citizens also vote without having a second thought on the name of Modi. They vote a candidate whom they even don't know. This creates a thinking in bjp leaders that they are always going to win the elections on the name of Modi. Yes, if citizens vote Modi in Lok Sabha elections, then it's not a problem as it is going to their desired leader which is not a problem. But the problem is that if citizens vote like this in local body elections to a candidate who may be corrupt is totally wrong. Citizens should not vote on the name of popular figure to any person whom they do not even know how he/she is. so, in local or legislative or central elections citizens should vote by seeing the candidate's personal deeds and not on which party he/she represents. Yes, this chapter is smaller compared to other chapters but it is important to choose a good leader not by his party but by his or hers work and image.

Ch. 9
All The Strengths and Weaknesses of our Country and How to Work on Them

Section 1: The Strengths of India

india has many strengths in this section I will talk about the major strengths' top strength of india is agriculture. India is a 'khati pradaan' or agricultural country which contributes 18% to our GDP or gross domestic product. India majorly earns by exporting grains to foreign countries by which we either get things, or money by the process called bi-lateral trading. The second biggest strength of india is our geographic location. India has a very strategic location which lies in the middle-southern part of Asia where India's map stretches from the mountains of Himalayas then passing by the heat of thar desert till the southern most parts of india like Kanyakumari. Almost all types of natural resources can be found in India, because of different geographic zones in India. The 70% of the water collection of Brahmaputra River is collected in the north-eastern boundaries which stays in Arunachal Pradesh, which also the biggest jealousy factor of China. The Himalayas and the deserts naturally create a boundary or a barrier for our enemies to reach India, by which it stays tough for our enemies to surpass the cold of Himalayas and extreme heat of Thar, which makes india secure. India also has its union territories like Lakshadweep and Andaman and Nicobar Islands. Who benefit india by giving us control over the 90% of the water trades from the most eastern parts of Asia, so the western and middle eastern Asia has a narrow-stretched trade route through Malacca path which connects east Asia with Europe and middle-east. The third and the last biggest strength of india is its youth population, where most of India's population stays under the age of 35, which creates a large amount of work force for India's development in various sectors. India has a long list of strengths and if I go to each one a whole book can be written on strengths of India, but these three were among the biggest strengths of india that's in olden days india used to be called 'sone ki chidia' or a golden bird.

Section 2: Weaknesses of India

India has many strengths which are gifted to us by God, but we have also created weaknesses by our own deeds. If I go to the major two weaknesses then the first among them lies, the health care issues. health care issues have rapidly grown in India due to expensive health care, as majorly all the hospitals stay private as a result most of the population cannot afford good health care facilities which also directly impacts on the youth or the work force of the country, however there are good government hospitals too, but they always have a great que because of which many people die in India who majorly stay labourers, workers etc. Which weakens the main strength of our country the working population. The second most weakness is corruption, this weakness stays the biggest one to contribute as a hurdle in most developmental progress of our country, where corruption stays to a very high percentage from 60% to 90% in each and every branch of government. Many schemes, bills are declared in many sectors like healthcare, education, infrastructure, road development, exportation and many more because of which sufficient amount of money doesn't reach to the population in need, which creates poor healthcare facilities, weak infrastructure, strikes by farmers, very low and least maintained amount of government schools etc. This creates a big problem for working population and overall developmental index of India.

Section 3: How to Overpower our Weaknesses

India has a great amount of strength as we discussed earlier but, these major weaknesses or flaws of our government creates a speed breaker for India's development.the first weakness as I have written earlier, is the health care issues. This weakness is integrated with the second and biggest weakness of India which is corruption so I don't have to discuss it seperately. to overpower corruption India needs to create very strict laws for the vigilance department and the civil servants, like death sentence for corruption because until leaders don't fear they will not stop. Some powers of the policeman and MPs should be restricted, and should only be given in rare situation if they are needed this permission should be directly given by judiciary's budget declared for any sort of scheme should be submitted to the supreme court and after their implementation, a supervision team with selected officers should be sent to supervise the expenditure of the money given in scheme whether the expenditure is accurate according to the budget allotted or not. And if not then all the involved officers, Las or any other government official should be sentenced in the court under revocation of their authority. All the government hospitals, schools should go under a supervision period every month so, that the infrastructural equipment stays under its excellent condition. India can do wonders without this dark spot of corruption on our face and we here to remove it from our country, if leaders fear then would not dare to misuse the money of citizens. Then only sovereignty of our country shall be maintained.

Ch. 10
An Ideal Way of Leading Bharat

so, at the last chapter of this book we have saw every aspect of India from starting till present, and also, we saw the solutions for problems.as 15 years old I know what is good and what is wrong for the government I am sure the leaders of our country too know. I am just an ordinary boy of the great country India who just wants to see India which is Bharat to grow. With this effort I will try to contribute in order to revolutionize our future in an excellent way. I think my effort will surely be heard to the government of india. so that future generations can see real superpower Bharat.

jai hind, Bharat Mata ki jay

Refrences of Leading Bharat

CHAPTER 1: REVOLT OF 1857; FROM THE NCERT TEXTBOOK OF 8TH GRADE

CHAPTER 2: FOREIGN POLICY ANALYSIS OF;UPA-INC GOVERNMENTS AND BJP-NDA GOVERNMENTS;FOREIGN POLICY AGENDAS FROM 1947-MAY 2014:EXAMPLES FROM 1988 military coup in Maldives from archives;1990 indo-sri lankan accord of from archives

CHAPTER 3: From the 1971 war archives;current analyisis of the operation sindoor and r&w warnings from ic 814 direct connection with terrorist attack warnings by r&aw : dev raval;leading bharat

CHAPTER 4: From the data of financial years 2009-2010;agenda analyisis of the financial policies of inc-upa government ;2004-2014: from data of financial years 2023-2025 present;agenda analyisis of the financial policies from bjp-nda government 2014-2025 at present

CHAPTER 5: “There are only 15 judges per million people”; THE ECONOMIC TIMES: 2025 india justice report; “ there are 47.44 million pending cases”: THE HINDU-THE CLOGGED OF INDIAN JUDICIERY;the Nirbhaya rape case;BBC “four men executed in delhi rape and murder case of 2012”

CHAPTER 6: Educational developments by the british rule and verneculer languages archives;working of Christian mischaneries and there education system: ncert 8th grade textbook of history

CHAPTER 7: According to the latest election system structure; “85 thousand duplicate voting”;from the press conference by opposition leader Rahul Gandhi; THE HINDU; “ED REGISTERS MONEY LAUNDERING CASE AGAINST SHIV SENA (UBT) MLA/MP RAVINDRA WAIKER”

www.ingramcontent.com/pod-product-compliance
Ingram Content Group UK Ltd.
Pitfield, Milton Keynes, MK11 3LW, UK
UKHW020051200726
13845UKWH00056B/806

9 788198 821454